To Vicki,
in admiration of
your wonderful
scholarship!

Sailing Lake Mareotis
EAMONN WALL

Eamonn Wall
Midwest ACIS 2016
Lawrence, KS.

salmonpoetry

Published in 2011 by
Salmon Poetry
Cliffs of Moher, County Clare, Ireland
Reprinted in 2013
Website: www.salmonpoetry.com
Email: info@salmonpoetry.com

ISBN 978-1-907056-85-7

COVER IMAGE: *Clouds and coastline* © *John Matzick* | *Dreamstime.com*
COVER DESIGN: *Siobhán Hutson*

PRINTED IN IRELAND BY SPRINT-print

Salmon Poetry receives financial support from
The Arts Council / An Chomhairle Ealaíon

To Matthew and Caitlin

Acknowledgements

Acknowledgments are due to the following publications in which some of the work included in this collection was originally published:

Agenda, Blue Canary, Scalder Verse / Enniscorthy Echo, Revival, Salamander, The SHOp, Turnrow.

Poems were also published in the following anthologies in Ireland and the United States and thanks are due to their editors.

Pat Boran. *Shine On: Irish Writers for Shine.* Dublin: Dedalus Press, 2011.

Matthew Freeman ed. *Flood Stage: An Anthology of Saint Louis Poets.* St. Louis: Walrus Publishing, 2010.

Jessie Lendennie ed. *Dogs Singing: A Tribute Anthology.* Cliffs of Moher: Salmon Publishing, 2010.

"The Pilgrims Emerge from the Forest" was commissioned for *Christmas Songs of Praise*, an ecumenical carol service held at St. Aidan's Cathedral, Enniscorthy, on December 12, 2010. This service concluded the year-long *Enniscorthy 1500* celebrations. Thanks to Fr. Denis Kelly Adm., St Aidan's Cathedral, who commissioned the poem, to Rev. Chris Long who read the poem at the service, and to Annette Wall. A limited edition broadside of the poem was published in 2011, designed and printed by Firecracker Press, St. Louis, Missouri, USA.

Many thanks to Drucilla Wall, Kevin Higgins, Susan Millar DuMars, and Daniel Tobin for insights and comments they provided on poems included in this collection. A special thanks to Jessie Lendennie and Siobhán Hutson at Salmon for their support over the years.

Such a dream of shifting images this world seems.

MATSUO BASHŌ *Narrow Road to the Interior*

Then rose the seed of Chaos, and of Night,
To blot out order, and extinguish light,
Of dull and venal a new world to mould,
And bring Saturnian days of lead and gold.

ALEXANDER POPE *The Dunciad, Book IV*

CONTENTS

PART THREE

PART FOUR

PART ONE

WAKING SOFTLY, TENNESSEE

How our soft themes attach themselves
to rivers, flood plains, deciduous brown
golding, bright autumnal sun buffed up.
Entering Tennessee again the heart tung-
able of breath step, tray of artichoke set
in a beige order, the red of wine stretched
out beyond to low brown hills where
a gathering held noon time's reins
offering praise, each child dabbing a patch
of colour to a fine-lined page. We ramble
along by an old river, old Mississippi,
her movement of herself no grand gesture
of narration but a dreamless, awkward,
majestic sleep somnambulation. By car
or climbing route to air from Memphis,
we might note, though cannot note, how
cold the kestrel's pointed, indigent recall.

THE FOUND WORLD

after Robin Robertson

(1)

We walked there once, late afternoon,
listening out for ancestors, timber wolves,
the heft and stroke of evergreens high above
the road in Carrigdoon. As I recall it now,
the red scarf about your neck was loosely tied,
bandana style, your boots were as scuffed
and dry as the old leaves you pushed into
the sheltered cracks along the roadway:
we were following songlines to Lough
Arrow. I imagined or remembered
that you held my hand and I understood
that it was to you alone, among the two of us,
that the great gift had been offered: first,
among your father's elderberries, and, later,
on a walk through the great oak woods
an hour's journey from your childhood
home where you heard the great hinges
among the high oaks hollow out a fugue.
Who were we that late afternoon in Sligo:
son and mother, husband and wife, a boy
being led through night and day by a light-
skinned blue-scarfed lady? It was as if
in childhood that a book had been passed
into your hands. You opened that book,
you quickly broke its code. I, on the other
hand, had been raised among believers
to kick out blindly all spring at bluebells
and communists, to slash at tree bark
with a heavy hatchet stolen from
a neighbour's shed. I had no book. It was
not allowed. From a pulpit in the great
cathedral in my town, a clergyman,

gray and solid, paraphrased. I had been
trained to praise the heavens, hate all
that was natural to the world. The heart,
they reminded me, was a neutral zone.
As we walked, that afternoon under
Carrigdoon, you pointed out names
of what comprised this space, and these
I quickly memorized. At times, as we
walked, I clutched more firmly to your
hand. Then, as though some cherry picker
had raised me upward, I kissed the crows'
feet near your eyes. Your voice mesmerized
me. We walked on along a country road.

(2)

Save for map, crucifix and sacred heart,
our schoolroom walls stood naked.
In those forbidding rooms, we learned
of natural science that our world had
been formed by miracle that was full-
accounted in a book of truths we were
not allowed to read. As we walked
together on the paths below Carrigdoon
that afternoon, I repeated after you:
lady's bedstraw, fairy foxglove, salmon-
berry, meadow buttercup and royal fern.
As a schoolboy, I thought it a shameful
thing that my father could tell the songs
of birds and wished him silent when he
began to cite their names: first, in Irish;
then, reluctantly, in English, the language
more distant from his heart. I wanted
to say to you that had the schoolroom's
walls been decorated with scenes
from nature and schoolboys' art, I might
have accepted then the beauty of our

world and loved my father a little more.
I did not know that goat's-beard and field
forget-me-not were the wheelbarrows
on which our world depended, that history
was a patriot game written on the sands.

(3)

In Sligo, while you pulled me along
with your gentle teacher's measure,
I picked in a quiet manner among
an abundance of flowers and greens,
each placed in the left breast pocket
of my yellow *North Face* shirt. When
I got home, I lined my collection up
in a child's copy book, then sought
each Christian name out on the internet.

(4)

We left the road that ran parallel
to the lake and turned down a bohreen
whose ditches were all wildly overgrown,
whose stony centre shot up tufts of grass
and dried moss. We were walking
through the heart of deepest fairyland.
You liked to listen and I fell quiet too
for I thought to learn what listening was.
The sun retained its summer heat
though at times, when it clouded, a dark
hand reached across the little road. Step
by step we walked the wind rose, the wind
as quickly died way. I remember
a tractor's roar carried across the lake
like a booming cannon, clouds forming
above Carrigdoon. Walking, I learned
to fear no longer, all about us,

the darkness that shapes this world.
Absorbing, filtering, you walked to where
the road divided another time. There,
I was led inland by my returned father
and away from you. He had a list
for me, birds in Irish, and each word
I repeated after him: seabhac mara,
fuiseóg, préachán dubh, géis, gabhlán
gaoithe, caislín dearg. Good man,
he said, now I'll lead you home. The path
split again, narrowed, ended at a gate
and stile. We crossed a field, mounted
another stile, entered a stony yard. Ahead,
I saw that you were seated on a wooden
form, drinking coffee. My father said,
your children are inside. Before releasing
my hand to send me forward, he said:
a decade ago, you looked across this lake,
then back toward land, high woodland
overhead in Carrigdoon. You found in pine
needles the spot to hide your oar. Father,
I replied, though I believe you, I have
no memory of this. Son, you must stay
here. Learn the root names of this world
you share. Test against nature's truer ring,
old grunts that hollow square of wisdom.
But don't conceal yourself: you must
walk laneways to join those gathered
at each noisy crossroad: hear the roar
of the accordion, the pitch of an angel's
voice. Help us recover what has been lost,
help the young teacher fresh from training
college bluetack posters to her schoolroom
wall. My father, as is now his wont, was
one moment speaking, the next quite
vanished into air. She looked up shielding
her eyes from the sun as I approached her
wooden chair. Here, she said. We're here.

RETURN TO CHARLESTON

Long ago, so it seems that way, we ate
      —mother, father, son—
on these floating spaces. Each breakfast

then, as the tide rose daily to your knees,
      scaweed wrapped
itself about your locks, the smoothest

Of rubbed stones gathering themselves
      about your feet.
Today, on this public seat, I dumbly sit

Among old friends, cormorants & gulls,
      as vast crowds
cast from a docked ship queue to mount

A fleet of idled coaches, in observation.
      Cormorant that day,
A word our child tried desperately to say.

LAKESIDE FALLING, CO. SLIGO

I was astonished, too, at the impressive, clear beauty of the country and its variety, the amazing light and the sway of its healing and collusive charm.

PATRICK LEIGH FERMOR *A Time of Gifts*

1.

Look at the lake.

Point out the lopped hemlocks.

Observe our full moon hanging in a pine's curve.

2.

June on Lough Arrow. Two swallows
forage for flies. All of our origins dot,

breast-like & tomb-like, this old land:
Carrowmore, Labby Rock, Cromlech,

many acreages of sleep on the hillsides,
a cloudburst popping the sheds at dawn.

3.

The fox turned its back to the lake.
The wind did not bother the slipway.

We debated the merits of turquoise.
The evening was gray and the water was cold.

Rain fell from the edges of sheds. The white
rabbit pounded the perimeters of its cage.

4.

The moon illuminated the lake. The trout were in motion.

I asked for your hand and the sound of your voice.

The love of your children, the moor hen's refrain.

A LIFE OF PAT THE SCRUFF, CHAPTER 12

Somewhere on the road from St. Louis to Kansas City, my master, or that was how he saw it, keeled over.

He hit the ground with a dull thud that rose the dust into a light cloud, the sun high in the July sky. A goner!

We were on the Katy Trail, the quite interminable path that replaced a good Missouri railway line—designed for cyclists, walkers, the young and old. For dogs, recreational walking is a definite non-starter. We prefer to ride.

The trail we walked that day was cris-crossed by shadows cast from a long line of poplars, a legacy of Governor Ashcroft, the evangelist. Once, to an admiring crowd, we had heard the great man sing at an out-of-doors Springfield soiree. My master thought him an improvement on Andy Williams, a crooner he had lately heard in Branson, an evening I spent under a porch sheltering from driving rain and violent thunder. A man's life!

My name, they say, is Pat the Scruff or Scruff the Mutt. I eyed the heap in front of me. A light twig had blown into his pants' fold, his pack had rolled harmlessly to the path side. For once he did not jabber. On a fence post a blue jay stood, but I knew better than to bother with a bird. I took to pondering my situation.

Nearby, I heard a creek's flow though in no direction could I discern the voice of dog or man. For some, the middle of Missouri can feel like the middle of nowhere. For me, as I look back, it was heaven. To the best of my knowledge, I have never left the state. My master, he was fond of telling strangers, was a direct descendent of Mark Twain. I was on the verge of something great.

He had many sayings. His favourite was one attributed to Harry Truman. It goes, "If you want a friend in Washington, get yourself a dog." My master, or ex, would repeat this to me before beating me about the nose with the *Kansas City Star*. Who is a dog's best friend?

"Love the One You're With" is an old time song he liked to holler. That day, along the Katy Trail, I took that song's message to my heart. Moving on, certain I would be befriended soon along the way. In case my old man was merely sleeping, I stepped lively. A gentle breeze blew across the Katy Trail.

Who can resist a dog in uniform! To serve the Missouri Highway Patrol had for long been the most earnest of my desires. For many years I had dreamed of riding on a cruiser's soft leather as my partner at the wheel chased, in hot pursuit, packs of dirtbags and hardened criminals. In my heart, I have always felt the siren's wail. Little did I know, that day in mid-Missouri, that those dreams were about to be realized.

THE EMIGRANT RETURNS TO THE CAPITAL

I am walking through your city
late this Sunday afternoon
among many joyful football
flag wavers who hail from all
four corners of the nation.
They, knotted immodestly
into a tidal wave, push though
alleys and avenues kicking at
soda cans, driving children
deep into the hearts of ice-cream
parlours where gangly and tall
postcard stands shake terrified.
An old shopkeeper—he is burly
and severe—disturbed by this
sudden draft of wind, looks
outward, then, absentmindedly,
leans a great hand to soothe
his rattled children on display.
We are bound for an instant
when his eye locks on mine.
There, there, he whispers
to his Irish views. Fixed on
me, he notes my green shoes,
my traitorous *Herald Tribune*.

I am walking through your city
late this Sunday afternoon:
I had no side to take nor
team to cheer in the great
battles lately fought
at the sublime new stadium.
There's no banner to hold
my colours, no head to sport

the cap of my home place
though I, like many others
that you will meet on summer
Sundays in the capital, once
owed allegiance to a county
and followed in a mighty wave
heaves of expectant partisans
who had gathered to call your
name. Though it has of late
been modernized, the county
I recall remains as a dark
village in an old country,
faraway down an unpaved
road that nightly I negotiate,
my book set on the bedside
table, the lamp turned off,
city lights slowly settling
to my depth of sight. I listen
for the tap-tap of my father's
blackthorn stick on uneven
paving stones. Overseas.

I am walking through your city
late this Sunday afternoon:
it is the capital of a country
I had once known as home.
Once settled on a city trolley,
the flag wavers break into
tribal song as they seek to lift
the city on the tidal wave
they drive. *Sotto voce*,
I sing along though when seats
are freed at the next stop,
I do not seek a place among
these well-oiled baritones.
Instead, I wedge myself
between two families who,

as I suppose, have arrived
from Poland and Cameroon.
Though I have made my home,
these many decades now,
among foreigners, the seated
fathers on this city trolley,
left and right of me, fix me
with their wariest and most
distrustful eyes. I look out
the window. A neutral posture
of a visitor is now assumed.

THE LAST CRICKET OF THE SEASON

after Elizabeth Bishop

When I catch a cricket's high
autumnal pitch sprung from
among a row of ragged junipers,
my heart seeks out the levelest
and most insistent, homeward
foot and yard to my front door.
On Missouri's warmest days,
these many free and careless
years, I have often paused for
shade under a great oak tree
to observe pairs of doves that
quietly group under this same
line of evergreens. My children
have grown and spread, my
sweetheart is at home stirring
alone a late martini, and cars
roar to the westward freeway
bound for glory and California:
I grow invisible or gray which
is just the same difference as
they say. But this cricket's call
rocks my world—Jimi Hendrix,
Rolling Stones. Though cold
and colder this evening's air, I
can still pitch high, and I can
swing homeward, as if immortal.

THREE ROCK CANDY MOUNTAIN ORAL
MESSAGES: AFTER FERLINGHETTI

1.

The foreign national
I'd been sent
to shadow
from the margins
of the city
for a day—
we were camped
on Three Rock
Candy Mountain—
rolled her cart
to the first carriage
of a halted train.
Westland Row
that for the profiled
patriot had been
renamed Pearse
before reverting—
one more time—
to its more ancient
imperial name.

I observed
a conductor hold
an electric door
for a foxy lady:
her robber baron
husband, as I
suspected, flung
golden parcels
as if through air.
Crowds eyed
with suspicion

my scarlet letter
though I owned
a pass allowing
access to the city
through certain
daylight hours.

The old capital
was loosed
by summer's sun
so newspapers
in punters' hands
creased more crisply.
Like Chinese
lanterns, starched
and bright business-
men's shirts alighted
from halted trains.
Nothing appeared
as hopeless as
Paddy O' Plank,
who made hay
for *The Dublin News*,
had assumed. Was
the sun going down
on the patriot game,
a nation's folly
slumping on Anglo
bankers' lithe, cold
and crooked nails?
One could not blame
horse Protestants
or bearded Shinners
this time. A busker
wrung from the
season's moving heart
a tune as desperate

as it was forlorn.
Was it earnest light
of evening, or love
or even Bongo
bursting through
from midfield intent
on goal for
Leix/for Ireland
that gave this earliest
of twilights worth
and luster, July
calling out in song
from sharpest corners
of Eastern shores
easy living/easier
listening melodies?

A boombox
hollered many
anthems of an age
I had paused today
to gauge, an off-
kilter Taoiseach
belting out come-all-
yiz from a corner
of a Galway stage.
Then the platform
cleared. An old city—
I thought of footfalls,
like quiet exiles
melting into silence—
resumed its docile
homey beat on corners
where babbling visitors
will not tread, hours
to go before the sun
sidled below distant

hills. Then, a dog's
bark and a child's
song, a couple walking
hand-in-hand through
the wooden archway
of an ancient bar.

O, remembered capital!
In olden times,
I walked out with
Attracta De Valera
Seapoint salt still
clinging to our arms:
headed for shandies
in the snug of Kehoe's.

II

I was making
stations of a city
I now followed
on the radio. At
one time Dublin
had counted me
a wit and spread
vague wisdom
I had coined across
innards of papers
and magazines.
I wrote of brown
envelopes, urban
grime. With an
idle pose, my
voice was raised
among Poolbeg St.
denizens to order
yet another round.

Sequential thinking,
it was noted,
not your forte
when I was fired.

A thud, a cleaner's
cart forced forward
the swinging door
of the janitor's
inner station
of Westland Row.
When she had
removed her gloves,
washed her arms
from elbows
to hands, clocked
her card, she left
the station
by descending
escalator, walking
through a wide front
door to the city
street. She melted
into bus seat plastic,
slipping home. She
read on the city's
streets absence
and opportunity.
A foreign national:
I followed her.

III

Earlier, daylight
broken, I had left our
camp on Three Rock
Candy Mountain,

crossed dewy fields
where ancestors lie,
and met the bus
where the road
forks: one leads
to the city while
the second curves
toward the interior
of the nation. I had
been sent as family
witness to glean
facts of alien life:
were they deviant
and strange or just
as odd and ordinary
as ourselves? I trailed
the woman, sought,
as she turned
for home, permission
to spend the evening
among her family.
Yes, we have been
expecting you, she
replied. Fragrant, so
polite, I was quite
surprised at first.
We sat together
in the kitchen:
father, mother, son
and visitor. Food
eaten, the boy's
exercises corrected,
light cleaning
completed, I knelt
to hear five decades
of the Rosary,
our mother tongues

colliding first
then melting slowly
into prayer. Looking
outward, I saw
through lace curtains
on Fairview Close
many working
indigenous televisions
most brightly lit
to *SKY.* On the sofa,
the Polish boy
was reading from
James Stephens'
The Crock of Gold.

At midnight,
I took leave:
thanking for her
hospitality the carriage
cleaner and her
husband who, rather
than speaking,
blinked his eyes
toward me
in the gesture
of the immigrant.

IV

I peeled
through late-night
limbo dancers,
and recalled how,
in the argot of our
own time, even
before the Celtic
Tiger growled,

we had been taught
to think carriage
cleaners skips or
even skivvies,
women in kitchen
coats with netted
hair rolling carts
across filthy
platforms of a nation.

V

Here's a little
of family history:
as fools and uncouth
agitators, we had
been banished
to the mountain
by *Flinty Flail.*
Do you recall
the Great Removal?
We had protested
outside the Dáil
when our parks
were covered with
concrete, our Liffey
topped with sludge.
My father had held
his rebel banner high.
One night,
in retaliation,
a herd of brown-
shirts came:
great floodlights
lit our streets
as we were marched
to waiting buses

in single file.
Our house
was given over
to loyal supporters,
dissent no longer
tolerated. Our nation
now a corporation
run by gangsters
that included
a gang of turnip
greens.

Singly, we might
return to shop
by day on city
streets: as a group
we were barred.
While, the night
of our removal,
our heels were
cooled under open
skies, obese men
were seated under
western tents.
A leader wielded
a fountain pen
as his acolytes
struck up another
verse of "Galway
Bay", all visible
for public view
on silver screens
mounted across
Dublin. Video
and soundtrack
of our departure.

VI

On Three Rock
Candy Mountain,
my family slept
cat-piled together
by the fire, by rest
all primed and food
prepared for my
account of foreign
folk at work and play.
My father, always
king of the quick
cliché would surely
be forced to say,
his chin raised
like a razor blade,
the more things
change the more
they stay the same.
Once Viking,
now a Pole,
perhaps tomorrow
a Mongolian
arrived in Dublin
with a role to play.
I imagined his
reaction walking
home. I was
nervous then: my
father treasures
the well-turned
tale's ring of truth,
hands raised
to a roaring fire.
He would surely roar:
Poles, mythology,

And prayer.
Quick, my faithful
son, take me
to their home.
From ourselves
alone, these
brave foreigners
will surely
deliver us.

PART TWO

THE PILGRIMS EMERGE FROM THE FOREST

Onset of evening. Exit the forest.
A band of pilgrims descending east-
Ward to the river, clambering over
Fording stones to pitch camp upward
On a rise. Later, round lighted fires,
This group from the western lands
Gathers to eat, sing, chant old
Songs and sacred psalms, and before
Laying themselves down to sleep
The pilgrims' fire is kindled high
For body heat, and to guide home-
Ward on their way those who have
Lighted out across the untamed
Lands. As they sleep, wolves emerge
From forest deep to guard the scene
While deer form a noble perimeter
To the south. Overhead, owls and
Hawks hold a watchful brief. And
Obscured farthest in woodland dark,
Bears stand guard while feigning
Sleep. In stygian pools salmon stall
As eels hug fast the lapping shore.
The river rocks on the ebbing tide.

Onset of Morning. Early awakening.
Senan walks downward to the river
Hearing from the forest a sonorous
Cacophony of song. Three hares
Observe him from a rock, two foxes
Are placed on a broken limb, and
Flocks of birds have traced a mighty
Circle in the sky. Senan knows last
Night's vision and this morning's

Show are the purest signs. He must
Bury his staff and woolen cloak. To
Found a church, build a town, lay
Some solid markers down—for it is
Time. He rouses his followers to clear
Rough ground and fell fine oak trees.
The river rocks on the gaining tide.

Towns are christened, rivers handed
Names and churches built of wood
Are burned to be replaced by stone:
The forest retreats to accommodate
The town. On the wind nowadays,
We hear still the breath of wolf, the
Breath of bear and deer, the breath of
Oak that carries home to us a whiff
Of history's odor and brightest spark,
And hawks are provided shelter still
In high steeples atop the churches
Of this town. Old streets carry tales
Told once again and then another
Time or two. From this patchwork
I can form a mother's face and
Father's hands, can't you? Vowed
To stability, community and place,
Senan sank deep sleepers in most
Cherished ground. Letters formed,
Names on parchment noted down.
The Slaney rocks on an ancient tide.

RETURNING TO THE CAPITAL

Cities, after all, are places of both eviction and sanctuary."
MARK MAZOWER. *Salonika: City of Ghosts*

Though the sun goes down, the path ahead
is clear, city lights point to many islands
of expectation—a waiting cable car,
an opened café beside a busy convenience store,
a lively downtown bar, a kiosk whose owner
smiles zestfully at all walkers crossing into
his radar field. It is a zone of hope in the tribal city:
tablecloth, bread, unfolded chairs, a waiter writing
in his order book your spoken words.
Your guest has placed her hands into a posture of denial,
screwed her face, laughed loudly as you complete
for her sentences to restore her ease. You note how
in the waiter's book of life words are stripped
of stress and *umlaut*, how among travelers
and cosmopolitans locals assume but walk-on
roles. For as long as you have lived, you have sensed
the limits of your wisdom though now, turning
toward sixty you note how much uncertainty
has helped you to uncover truths placed idly
under stones. It was decades ago when you loitered
by the bus shelter for the girl that did not show. Now,
yours is a bleached and softer voice while the city's
tone is tuneful to the heart, your guest's face just radiant.

THE MONASTERY BELL

i.m. Michael J. Wall

(1)

That monastery day, the ringing bell,
my weeping father walking toward his parked car
absent an effort made to wipe his face
so that, hitting light of afternoon's liquid air
to which our crosses have been nailed,
hitting the world's arc, that second
month of autumn, he was blinded to our long,
forlorn, unhappy measure of separation
that he was then of right age to comprehend.
We, father and son, we were blindsided
so that, in the broken future we would share
we would from that day on pause
at crossroads, unstable and ill-defined,
to greet. We would throng in spaces
where there could be no privacy:
on the bridge that carried travellers uphill
to Co. Carlow, your youngest sister
holding firmly to your hand as I climbed
an iron gate better to observe girls spinning
to banjo, fiddle and accordion. We might
idle together among fruit and vegetable stalls,
or shuffle down rows of Sunday-best suits
and dresses set for sale, hung on black racks
under heavy canvas sheets. Fair Day,
when all ecstatic breathing parts compete
for our attentions, under your mountains.
Above us the bones of our ancestors: peat-
softened under Mount Leinster's Nine Stones.

(2)

That monastery day, the ringing bell,
my weeping father, I have reached his age
for looking backward now: it is my time.
My father's car has pulled away, crossed
the cattle bars and I am headed to the chapel
for evening prayer when I am called, by the light
touch of his cold hand, to pause in the corridor
and face a window painted for St. Patrick.
The bell has wrung another time. I see
the hot stained glass of late liquid afternoon
set itself in motion as lake water can pulsate
toward waiting feet. Lakeshore in a light breeze,
captured in the frame I face, stained imperfectly
to life. In the window's tune of hours, the saint
moves toward the shoreline as a paschal flame,
as I suspect, gains traction on top
of a distant hill. A crowd gathered in a field,
many thousands as I assume, has raised
arms to shape, I can discern, some deep
shared gesture of greeting, ecstatically
unmeasured. You don't mean me,
I whisper to the glass, as packs of boys walk
behind me to the chapel of this monastery to hear
five decades of the rosary a millionth time?
Time is quite unstable and ill-defined.

(3)

Liquid light of afternoon, my father
walks across the gravel to his car, so I have
spun the clock backward into a yarn to peer
in that red lake scene, St. Patrick's window,
my father holding to my hand: together,
we await disembarkation of the saint.
A squall arises from the east that drives

the crowd toward shelter under trees
so that, shaded, dry, they can observe
St. Patrick's vessel turn to face the wind.
The hand that guides me to the glacial scene
is cold; quickly, the window folds
back to its fixed form. My father,
you now realize, is of late departed
from our world. Once the teenage boy,
walking to the chapel to pray, I had strained
to read two faces who stood to the edge
of the pilgrim crowd: my own and my father's
faces, by virtue of his passing on to his eternity
beyond Bunclody and the Blackstairs
Mountains, are now full, illuminated, finally
well-defined. He has joined his youngest
sister on the other side of time.

(4)

One night in deepest winter my father
called me out onto to the landing
of my American home. I found him seated
on a rocking chair, his radio tuned
to *NPR*. Through he held a rosary, he was not
then tuned-in to prayer; rather, he ran
the wooden pieces through his fingers
playfully to hold time as Frank Sinatra
sang. Outside, a north-west wind pushed,
with a scraping noise, honeysuckle limbs
against the wood frame exterior of my house
so that, listening and quite distracted,
I was reminded of Mr. Lockwood's first
night resident in "Wuthering Heights."
My father wore a three-piece pin-striped
suit, starched white shirt, his tie shaped
elegantly into a Windsor knot so that
everything of his bearing was as neat

and as precise as I would have expected
it to be. It was the middle of the night,
late-February, Missouri, I had been sleeping,
my family out-of-town, my father was
adjusting his radio to low. Three years ago,
he said, we spoke for an hour
about the monastery that day, the ringing
bell that pulled us apart like duelers
in a forlorn western scene. We spoke
of what you remembered, I reminded him,
and all I could recall and concluded,
both of us too shy to say, that neither
word nor silence divides us: naked,
we stand together on an open plain.
I have come to you, my father said,
to teach how the Windsor knot is tied
so that all will know how you are kin to me.
Quick, put an ironed shirt on, grab your ties:
I have but little time to linger in your lovely home.

FATHER SAVED BY DAUGHTER

When he shoulders his door this night
a rabbit scatters over crisp leaves
and dried carcasses of locusts & cicadas.

The ground tightens over bulbs sunk
and tuned in these long hours, toxins
aerate his century-old Missouri suburb.

Heavy as lead his hard-warped feet tap
trash to curbside. By sands, hydrangea,
and purple sage his girl's brown hair—

Reader, observe—is brushed by the West.
Wide-open windows on the second floor.

YOUR RIVERS HAVE TRAINED YOU

You've got to leave home.
You don't want to do it too soon.
Or leave it too long.

Your rivers have trained you,
Oceans prepared you.
Lakes have assumed you.

One night on Lough Arrow, as the boat closed-in
On the hump-backed bridge at the end of the channel,
You piloted me firmly to shore.

You've got to leave home.

You pointed to the cairn on the hill.
The moonlight patterned waters.
A flock of sheep grazing on a sloping field.

You don't want to do it too soon.

Hudson, Missouri, Mississippi: your rivers are majestic.
The Slaney has assumed your face's fair shape.
Jesus, see my shadow. My body is becoming air.

Or leave it too long.

Wrapped in blankets, you were soothed by the sea.
We watched behind poles put in place halting the tide's progress.
When night came in, I raised you above my head as comfort
    to cold stars.

Your rivers have trained you.
Oceans prepared you.
Lakes have assumed you.

You don't want to do it too soon.
Or leave it too long.

TORNADO ALLEY UNIVERSITY

But you have there the myth of the essential white America.
All the other stuff, the love, the democracy, the floundering
into lust, is a sort of by-play. The essential American soul is
hard, isolate, stoic, and a killer. It has never yet melted.

D. H. LAWRENCE *Studies in Classic American Literature*

All entreaties to seek shelter he had
Brushed aside. It was morning. The
Darkened sky had unraveled quickly
To tornado hue. At times, nightshift
Duties ended late, he would show-up
Uniformed to teach at eight a band
Of ragged students in pajama pants
And jeans. He specialized in the
Fictions of Owen Wister and Zane
Gray and liked to say that America's
Days of greatness had passed away.
Short of money, he took the extra
Job on account of sundry bills and
Student loans he was forced to pay.
Worked security for ZZT Solutions.

The sky grew darker, sirens growled.

He was the single man set solo against
Our world. He perched himself among
Our building's ancient rafters sure as
An old bell ringer in an Eastwood film.
We left him there, the boss of our dept.,
Holding his gun, and we descended as
A group to abide one another's company
In our building's basement. Each, in his
Or her own way, belonging to the un-

Requited heart of tornado alley, I thought
It prescient that none down here bore
Revolvers or blades concealed. Going
Postal: No, No, No! An hour to Mid-
Western lunch: tombed, and I was
Ravenous for my plate of bread, my
Square of cheese at sirens' end. Though
It's now forbidden, the man upstairs,
We all suspected, must surely light a
Cigarette. Freed at last by prevailing
Winds, pushing the storm eastward to
Iowa, we found our senior colleague
—Virginian. Aristocrat of Violence—
Blowing rings. His revolver rested
coldly between L'Amour's *Hills of*
Homicide and James Joyce's *Ulysses*.

IN MY FIAT BAMBINO

In my silver-winged Fiat Bambino, I soared high above Webster Groves. All the lovely azaleas on Newport arched toward hostas and rhododendrons—the latter, I noticed, no longer knotted tight from winter's freeze. On Glen Road arrays of daffodils marked spaces like children's heels dug into flannel sheets one winter's night when ice pellets ticked old-clock-like at window glass. I reveled in wild colour and suburban order: all the boy trees on Marshall were idly dressed in J. Crew pants and Ralph Lauren shirts.

Landing on the roof of Avery Elementary, I quickly released the children from the tedium of decimals and science; for sure, there would be no further crude parsings or dumb humiliations this day. Hands up all who want out, I announced. The tannoy carried my voice throughout red-bricked buildings and Quonset huts. I bore witness to stressed-out office staff answering emails and responding to nuisance calls. When the Diet Coke ran out, the school would have to run on empty.

On foot the children followed me to the St. Louis Bread Co. where we formed a mighty line for soups, sandwiches, and salads. When the police, supported by three county fire departments, arrived to supervise the crowded scene they were royally treated to Frontega chicken lunches and the strongest coffee. Around one great table, those in uniform shared many tales of bravery and guile. And vigilance is our motto, a sergeant boomed across the crowded space.

When Indians arrived fresh from retracing family steps made along the trail of tears, the teachers put mounds of permission slips to one side and offered to hold the Osage horses, tired from many hours negotiating Big Bend Blvd. A Clayton matron upon entering Straub's supermarket complained to the manager about the great commotion taking place outside. She was quickly offered a tub of chicken salad and California cabernet, and, in a flash, her anger was defused.

Back at Avery, the principal and custodian searched on hands and knees for dropped quarters in quiet rooms while at the Bread Co. the children were growing restless. Stay away from school, I said. Is it not all violent and grave? On the contrary, a bright girl said, it's so much fun. Later today, we have show-and-tell and I can't wait to commence our latest Science lesson. Yes, they all cheered in happy unison, show-and-tell and then an hour of snakes and crocodiles. In my day, I was forced to say, we thought our teachers the only reptiles present in our town. Oh dear, a confident boy piped up—while pointing toward my Fiat Bambino—the schools did really suck in Outer Space, I guess.

Outside, we shook hands before separating. From a height, I followed a wave of children down Lockwood Avenue where I gestured at them all my fondest farewell. In the distance Old Glory flew majestic above Avery Elementary. I turned suddenly to the north anxious to reach by nightfall Gander's famed Albatross Hotel.

CBS: ONE MORNING IN A CAFÉ IN DENVER BREAKFAST HOUR

A gray man seats himself beside me. Says it's
OK, I am not about to place my hand discreetly
Upon your knee. Perhaps, out of context, you
No longer remember me. Decades have passed

Since you broke from school for good to hit the
Outbound Road. I watched you among a group
Of boys headed riverward. Look now: here you
Are perched, my soft parakeet, eavesdropping

Among foreigners in this fearsome land. Your
Teacher of olden times, I counted individually
And as a group: boys setting forth on the dusty
Road of life. Sleepy Valley CBS to immortality!

As you well know, the gray man says, I battered
You until the slide-rule broke and, then, I tended
Just a little more for you showed high disregard
For school equipment. I was Risteard McDaniel

Then, a holy man who gaily learned you how to
Hate your town, who grafted to your waking soul
Guilt of long-dead generations and taught you
Where in your heart to harbor best an ounce of

Deepest shame. When it was whispered to me
On the street by your Uncle Tom that you liked
To sit at night alone upstairs, that you had lost
Your will to play, I rubbed hands again and I

Called it fairness found. Those were joyful days
When I ruled the roosts and minds of the rural
Lands. Once, I recall, the boys departed for the
Day, your uncle passed across my desk one full

Carton of Afton Major cigarettes with a gracious
Smile for all I had done to further our nationalist
Revolution. Educated youth, mailboats leaving
Ireland empty for the English coast, Fr. Murphy,

The Croppy Boy and P. H. Pearse, all and sundry
Bunk that passed for wisdom then. Always at our
Door—harridan, weak, half-educated of the town
—bearing hams, potatoes, loaves of soda bread.

Averting his eyes, this gray man who has taken a
Seat beside me in a Denver café, spoons sugar into
His milky tea. He spreads a packet of Smucker's
Strawberry jam across a slice of pumpernickel

Toast. Your father, he resumes, led the Burntown
Pipers across Old Town Square; he died abroad
On holidays in a hired car; your mother Lily, an
O'Brien from Tullamore, God rest her soul, of

Angina passed away a year or two ago. I am still
Abreast of the Irish news. Then, the gray man
Breaks to survey this day in Denver the passing
Breakfast hour: the messenger boys, secretaries

In flight, small groups of lawyers from courthouse
Broken free. Idly, he is involved in private conver-
Sations in the manner of a man who had given
Many years of life to teaching. Eating all the while

Most blindly with great energy; steady-handed,
Still clear-eyed, haircut fit for Armed Forces USA.
Brother McDaniel, I sure as hell remember you.
That day you mention, I walked halfway to the

River before turning right-handed toward the
Railway station. I left town, hiding in the bolted
Jacks as Jimmy Joe, the old conductor, made his
Rounds. Indeed, it's true, we all remember you

Though I must say that long ago I rubbed clear
The poisoned slate you passed into my satchel.
Tabula rasa it read when I looked at it in Liverpool.
A hippy chick I knew in Andalucía nailed it above

Her poodle's bed. Brother, you beat us and you
Held us down. Indeed we shriveled when you
Cursed our town out loud. We learned by rote,
Our brows burrowed into frowns. All that irony

And sarcasm—this wisdom you possess—has
Long time passed from me. We are remnants
Of the town we knew together but did not share.
My stomach was gripped by fire then drought,

I lay awake at night. I did not howl. I was not
Branded someone special for, luckily, this fate
Of mine was shared by all. Marked us all: but
At home our names were added to the pot. Our

Mothers ladled soup from pot to plate: at table
End we waited portions to wend a way into
Our hands. We banged our spoons in unison on
The wooden board, sang rebel songs before an

Open fire. To confirm a niche among an ancient
People, my grandfather placed his hands upon
My crown of curls. He lit his pipe and cursed
Our government. He then aimed a mighty hock

Toward the roaring fire. Br. McDaniel eyes a
Line of locals as they pay for items in this sultry
Denver café, smiling at me with undisguised
Contempt. Too long the prophet to hear me out.

Time moves on, I say, we drift away from deeply
Planted rages, that handiwork of yours, the seed
Money you had spent. Alighting from planes,
We step among faces to learn new names, learn

Strategies to confront grey men who walk like
Shadows across our days. Today, I barely know
That nation you have so dumbly described. Each
Of us walked from the temple as another child.

Well said, my parakeet, what you lack in brains
And sense you make up with the finest rhetoric.
I am Realtor Skip James nowadays, a part-time
preacher Elmer Gantry of the Rockies and High

Plains on the side. A decade wed to Betty Anne,
Great little ride, two girls home-schooled hard
On the edge of Denver upscale subdivision name
Of Somerset. Here's my card: you might well be

Interested in property or salvation. Six on each
Hand, I wielded the leather high and hard on all
Schoolboys' palms, the locals called our school
The Slaughterhouse. Was it as good as sex? I bet

You'd like to know. The speaker places his hand
On top of mine. It is easier to assent to unwonted
Tenderness than resist. My parakeet, he resumes,
Both of us departed a busted land. Our lot knew

The game was up before the axe had time to fall.
We pocketed our coins and confronted the Out-
Ward Road. In Dublin Airport, I flung my collar
And rosary beads into a Departures' garbage can.

As you will have guessed I vote Republican. My
Glock these days scatters cans across the semi-
Arid wastes of Colorado. Are not we, gathered
Here, men of accomplishment and great content?

Elbows planted and palms raised toward me that
Gesture: do not dare to make a word of answer.
He stands, turns, exits through a revolving door.
One morning in a café in Denver. Breakfast hour.

PART THREE

AUBADE CRACKED ALONG THE EDGE OF IOWA

*I was worried about my plans. With every pilgrimage one
encounters the temporality of life. To die along the road is
destiny. Or so I told myself. I stiffened my will and, once
resolute, crossed Ōkido Barrier in Date Province.*

MATSUO BASHŌ. *Narrow Road to the Interior.*
Trans.Sam Hamill.

We ate alongside Highway 61, watched the rusted Silverado
Lead along a John Deere harvester. A morning cruiser trailed.

Golden companion's head of hair, her plate of Perkins' eggs
And toast I read. She ate slowly, stiffening against the road.

She pointed across early spring snow melt vista at two men,
Though, at first, only Sora was visible to me. They climbed

Three concrete barriers, these visitors from Japan, crossed
A culvert astride a subdivision of millennial homes, affixed

In haste to heartland earth. Mexicans, a Cubs-hatted-man
In a nearby booth intoned toward Matsuo Bashō and Dora,

His loyal companion, southward walking a narrow path hard
To the edge of Iowa. Bilious in season my Mississippi heaved

Hosomichi road. I, too, had seemed that visitor once and have
Retained stranger's dust hidden under finger nail and in each

And every trouser fold. Wordlessly, we had hauled our packed
Bags down hotel corridor and winding stair. A smiling clerk

Was seated midst Keokuk bric-a-brac. For safety in Missouri,
Matsuo Bashō and Dora were clad in military fatigues as they

Exited at first light sedate and ordered Iowa. My companion is
My wife of many years. Old Glory is raised outside our home.

"To Die Along the Highway" Bashō had heard a crooner sing
In a sparse Minnesota tavern. Now he was hitting stride on a

Narrow path to Bourbon St., many days of trekking to the south.
She asked, "Did you have a good time last night?" "Yes," I did

Reply. Keokuk, Ft. Madison, Burlington, Davenport, Dubuque
Are the names of towns we saw as we followed the homeward

River slow. Shyly, just an hour ago, like young lovers, we had
Walked across the parking lot of the Comfort Inn to our parked

Sedan. "*Hsin*", you said. To which "*Kokoro*" was my reply.
At last, shifting reaches emptied into white sheets and broken

Blinds as the great Mississippi empties daily onward to the Gulf.
She reminded me, because I had fallen another time to staring

And confusion: you were one raised by a river of narrow faces,
The pinched preachers battered hard. A winter's morning, was

My reply, an *oku*-dead-end town on Europe's rainy edge. Your
Father, she said, is seated still on his sheltered bench riverside

And his is the face your weak eyes strain to hold. Matsuo Bashō
And Dora, it was my guess, had by now crossed into Missouri.

Morning had cracked my gaze. Of formality, my father's slate
Had been wiped clean though I followed still his light onward

To the promenade and felt, lightly, his right hand when it was
Placed upon my own left shoulder: We follow our rivers home.

A WINTER CALLER

She talked through a winter's day, the sun
        slanting over the dying mill,
of angled light on green water, ragged boys
        walking the railway line,
of one row of cups rinsed on white cloth, images
        speckled across the silent screen.

She said gulls circle where the river bends, at mid-
        season's point of light,
that gorged on rainfall and snowmelt, the river will
        run ponies to the roadside.
She tapped her ring on my cracked mug, the street
        lights burning up the gathered gloom.

Within the table's slatted octagon and sealed
        in her bubble
of familiarity, I was held. Her gaze passionate
        and firm. For many years
she had discounted the path I walked through blind
        alleys lined with beveled glass.

Elders spoke, the town retreated from view,
        my boat rounded river bends.
Yet she, the canvasser, returned with fresh leaflets
        and trill expectation
to catch me making rounds of neighbours' homes
        each winter yarn.

With slow purpose, she stirred the scattered dead
        beyond the pale
and struggled for directness, to recite what is well-known:
        how a town runs through
a walker's blood, its streets composing each facial line.
        Cups of tea, tales reprised, open door.

BILINGUAL DAY TRIPPER

*He was exact when he said a novel is not an argument
but an impression.*

CLAIRE TOMALIN. *Thomas Hardy*

I set out
from Helsinki—
Helsingfors to some—
switching at Karis—
perhaps Karjaa
to you. Headed
for Hanko, spa town
of old tsars and
point of departure—
Oh, broken infirm.
Onward to Hangö
ticket to ride. Exiles
all hurling, oceans
are wide.

I arrived
in Ekenás—
quite unwilling
to move—
where children
would dance before
tasting the rain.
Among buyers
and vendors—
quick market traverse—
a green archipelago
flung in front
of my eyes,
Tammisaari.

Linvävaregatan,
Hattmakaregatan,
Handskmakaregatan,
appeared on a map—
deadly as nightshade
milk for the newborn—
from weavers of linen,
the hatter and glover,
I found each street
bore an artisan's trade,
Ekenás.

I joined
youths for coffee—
that's lingua franca
on bright
formica.
They asked
first about Wichita
then Connemara.
So. I returned
to Helsinki—
Helsingfors to some—
switching at Karis—
perhaps Karjaa to you.
As Swedish
one's writ,
its comrade's all
Finnish.

A SORT OF CRUSADE

For every walk is a sort of crusade, preached by some Peter the Hermit in us, to go forth and reconquer this Holy Land from the hands of infidels.

HENRY DAVID THOREAU

This morning three orioles alarmed by my footsteps
Bolt from the maple that's third in a row between

Sidewalk and fence, all bordering Holy Redeemer's
Soccer field: it serves too as the winter patch where

Parishioners gather to purchase trees come Christ-
Mas time; filling, believers say, the pockets of the poor.

The product down the street, I have often noted, at
Freemasons' parking lot, near City Hall and Police

HQ, is more competitive as far as prices go, my
Own tree a wild Target perennial, I should add,

Purchased some years ago, if you must know, at the
Brentwood Promenade on the Feast of the Epiphany.

They did not favour Catholics—I mean Freemasons
And not the Target Corporation—we were often

Reminded while growing up in Ireland, one spacey
Nation hardly renowned for religious toleration.

I am enjoying a ramble through Webster Groves, soft
Tree city, bucolic heartbeat of St. Louis County as

Bells sound ten. Workmen from Tony's Tree Service,
Immigrants like me, labour busily under the earnest eye

Of Holy Redeemer's pastor. I want to shout out to Fr.
Andy that I was a Catholic for Kerry in '04. I defied

Your angry boss, Archbishop Raymond Burke, & for
All dire warnings, have not been torched by lightning

Bolts. However, well-brought up though hardly humble,
I resist the devil's temptation to harangue. With lengths

Of rope and roaring saws, the men work efficiently on,
Moving in manly rhythms. Their gaffer drags hard

On an unfiltered cigarette, shaded, idle, to one side.
I walk on toward Old Orchard admiring great oaks

And curved paths, the ordered to and fro of Eden
Seminary where matters of theology are solved by

Walking and end my reverie where Bompart and
Lockwood Avenues intersect. The High School

Band has broken camp in Hannibal. Our daughter
Is by now en route to her old shingles and mocking

Birds. Having turned northward toward home,
I choke this crusading spirit of my morning walk.

From a great distance, urgent voices call my name:
Each seeks a song of gin, gore, highwaymen profane.

MILWAUKEE, BE A SONGSTER

i.m. James Liddy

1.

He was wildly raised among the sidhe of Corca Bascinn
and rebel monks settled hourly at Glenstal
emerging green-clothed to parade
down Oakland Avenue toward Axel's Bar.
Child and changling. Child again alert
to anti-Treaty moralizers loitering
through the snowy diasporic alleyways of the East Side.

2.

In rain outside Co. Clare, a low group stood to receive
one aphorism as buses passed like ships at sea,
as scouting waves caught the air
and nearby froze to old Lake Michigan, as in lamped
North Shore homes proper folk dulled toward
asphyxiation, knots wound to swollen groins
only poetry could undo, could fashion to crocus,
rose or daffodil. Emerging through the doors on the highest
step, the poet's tongue lit by *abergut* intoned,
"The cold air of the violins kept the swans off the lake."

3.

Outside deep-dark O' Rafferty's the owner's son swept
butts and matches gutterward. Across the street
a meitheal of council workers broke stones.
Inside, at a table by the fire, Vincent O'Rafferty
polished the accordion on which everything
depended. Each morning, the poet kissed his mother, set out
from the doctor's house to cajole onto his wavelength

a dormant world, walking a path across hoar frost fields,
the many folk he met along the way.
I thought him Peter Pan though he did not consider
himself immortal in that sense though many were sure
he could be numbered so with Patrick Kavanagh and Oscar Wilde.

4.

From morning fog, blue mountains emerge.
White clouds drift inland from the Irish Sea.
The blank limestone is arroyo-lined
and sheep graze throughout the model range.
In threadbare jackets, baseball hats and hobnailed boots,
a band of pikemen in defeat descend a freshly tarmacadamed road.
They stop outside the poet's house to sing in strongest voices
their most glorious, tattered songs. "The high school band
was legendary" is the poet's most joyful refrain.

EVENING ON A BACK ROAD

Scattered sheets of cloud and a late burst of sunlight
tangle with tree limb and oak leaf between the seaside

and Camolin. I drive blinded again on the back road
by an old sun falling away to the Blackstairs' mast.

For all these years along this route, I have called out
to a fat church spire at the end of a line of yew trees

that never could despoil the ripened shamelessness
of fields bedded on layers of wet marl. Beasts heave

and breathe, the road bends over the humped bridge.
This road is within me, so blindly drifting: it is itself

& the wind's lone gray substitute, as full of movement
as the railway's sleepers are dipped in creosote and

fixed to a narrow gauge. Cows swing from the church
bell's rope. Sugar beets bolt from the ground. As the

strawberry absorbs the dew, the widower discounts
the news. The priest's housekeeper has turned-up his

stereo to twenty-five. Meeting the River Bann at the
main road, I pick from neon each yellow of the village:

A petrol station, Wexford flags, and the Parkside Bar.
So then! The road straightens. The car picks up speed.

SNOW FALLING ON OPENING DAY

I

Two brothers dressed to play today
Stand disconsolate, faces pressed
To deep-plated supermarket glass
As snow falls generously to asphalt,
Cars, and ambulance. I pass by, pull
A grocery cart—one among many—
From Schnuck's Brentwood atrium.

There's a spillage on aisle thirteen:
It notes all lost days are not erased.

II

I walk hand-in-hand down the stony
Lane, mother dressed in her floral
Summer dress, singing, as she often
Sang, "These Foolish Things," that
Song I had once thought, as I pulled
Queen Anne's Lace and fuchsia
From the hedgerows, she had made
For me, her fingers tinkling idly
On the grand piano of her failing
Heart. When that last July at sun-
Down she sought among new arrivals
At the commissary some news from
Town. And bread, milk, cigarettes,
And wine. She sat among women
Till shutters were drawn down, all
Huddled into cardigans. A lover,
Feverish and severe among school
Children, I feigned the mildest play.

III

Two brothers—the first an Albert
Pujols, the second a smaller Adam
Wainwright—pull plastic sleds, all
Red and white, across the pristine
Parking lot. Claiming the space at
Schnuck's entrance the baseball boys
Had held, I shape through wiped
Plate glass the narrow lane to which
Mother and son adhered. The boy,
Among grey hedgerows, is caught
Breaking from his mother's vocal
Grasp, while the scene itself begins
Its shift toward formlessness. We
Would sit on stormy evenings with
Our opened books, television wiped
Out by the wind, white lines across
A dark background. Who read at
The kitchen table, which one of us
Slouched in a brown armchair?

IV

Inside the bright commissary, where
Forms were placed in front of wooden
Shelves, a man stood before his dry
Goods singing. His arms opened into
A torc of welcome when a customer
Entered from the lane. A bell rang.

V

Too heavy with breath and memory,
The supermarket window moistens
Over. The two boys have long since
Departed for, as I imagine, the Art
Hill ski slope in the family minivan.
On Brentwood Ave., across from
Where I stand, this late-March day,
Buses pass and falling snow catches
To mother's hair: such foolish things
As time procures. I am looking
At my pasted breath, seeing nothing.

SAILING LAKE MAREOTIS

The Saturday world glides as I look toward Seth Child Rd. I am eating breakfast at Panera Bread: plain bagel, coffee in a paper cup. Throughout the café and parking lot, this bright late-October morning, home-comers in Wildcat purple are assembling in great numbers to rehearse the K-State battle song.

In a little while, breakfast over with, boozy tailgate parties winding down, a momentous battle, greater than Agincourt, will take place: the homecoming football game is scheduled for early afternoon at Bill Snyder Family Football Stadium: Kansas State Wildcats versus the Cyclones of Iowa State.

I am in Manhattan, KS, "the Little Apple", this weekend to visit my youngest child who is a student here. Loyal to a T, I have pinned my hopes on the Kansas State football team though the inner workings of the game are a source of some confusion to me.

This is the middle of the Flint Hills, a sacred place as I have learned from PrairyErth, at the centre of a vast and confusing country called the United States of America. Rest assured that I am a citizen though when I say this to people they do not tend to heed me.

The hills roll gently here, there is an ease in how the local people walk, the air is crisp, the light is fixed and fine. A country person myself, I find myself among my own kind. On my way here this morning, I saw a coyote wandering the edge of a cut-corn field.

Exiting the café by the rear door, I cross the parking lot to join a group of men and women gathered in front of a row of dumpsters to which the title of Midwest Waste has been conferred. They are all drinking: some coffee from paper cups, others soda pop from aluminum cans.

After presenting my credentials—immigrant from Ireland—they smile, relax, resume their conversations. I join a man from Honduras: we speak of home, family, work, green cards, Homeland Security raids. When I note that there exists no such person, in my view, as the illegal alien, he does not disagree.

Three women join the group on break from work: a Filipino, a Bosnian, and an older woman from Quito, Ecuador, who is given a red milk crate to sit down on. Her husband is a roofing company supervisor, she tells me, while she herself has been making Mexican tacos these twenty-seven years in Kansas and Missouri.

Finding a second crate, I seat myself beside Maria Dolores Suarez. She explains how in ancient times, more than is the case today, Lake Mareotis separated Alexandria from Egypt, and that Alexandria, as Michael Haag has pointed out, "was *ad* and not *in* Aegyptum."

She recounts for me sundry facts concerning the history of the area that surrounds Alexandria, points out how the lake itself was degraded, drained, and then brought back to life, at least to some degree, in recent times.

Many of the terms she provides I have not heard of and, therefore, do not understand: Maks, Kingdom of the Harpoon, Tehenu and Naukratis are a few I can recall. No, I reply to her query, I have not heard of St. Menas. I fill my pipe another time.

An old sailor, settled in Quito, as far away from the sea as he could be, would sit after dinner with my father in the white courtyard at our building's core. As they smoked their cigars, the sailor often spoke of Egypt. A child, she recalls, I sat in the shadows listening; my job to fetch coffee when my father raised an arm.

As immigrants, Maria Dolores Suarez says to me, we pass our lifetimes sailing Lake Mareotis. On a light craft, each of us has left Alexandria for Egypt. Our journey occurs in ancient times when the region was known to Virgil for the excellence of its wines.

75

Lake Mareotis is vibrant, stretching far away toward distant sands. We approach the mainland without ever arriving. On our approach, the land effects the smoothest of turns away from us, like a lover shifting away from one considered lame. We are in the United States—it is undeniable—though we are not of it.

As a wise man wrote not so long ago, no matter where we settle, we will all go gray walking along our childhood avenues. Both the Alexandria we have departed from and the Egypt we approach are visible and lighted. However, we do not ever exit Lake Mareotis, Maria Dolores Suarez concludes.

A man, bearing a television set, emerges from the rear of Wendy's. Behind him a long electric cable stretches back into his place of employment. He is greeted fondly by the gathered crowd. When he has settled it properly on top of a dumpster, the new arrival turns the television on.

A reprise of the recent El Clásico from the Bernabeu is about to commence: Real Madrid versus Barcelona. Look, Maria Dolores Suarez from Quito, Ecuador, shouts to her two lady companions, there's my man, sexy Javier Mascherano from Argentina.

We watch the game together—quietly, intently—called back onto a familiar stage, a warm curtain drawn between us and the United States.

Throwing my cup into the dumpster, I wave goodbye and take the longer route round to the front entrance of Panera Bread and, once there, hold the door for a long line of exiting Wildcat fans. Big 12 Football. Homecoming game.

To a man, woman, and child they are happy, warm, friendly, purple and appreciative of my quiet gesture. You are welcome, I say, and good luck against Iowa State today. In the café, I order two hot breakfasts-to-go for my wife and daughter who will surely have woken-up by now. Go Wildcats!

SUMMER STORM MISSOURI

Sheet swept
bleach rain
parkland
drone:
downward
windward
chair-o-plane.

PART FOUR

ACTAEON'S RETURN

At a time in the future, on a bus headed for the Southeast, Conleth Doyle seats himself beside Actaeon O'Neill. Citizens are now allowed to return to their home towns on day trips. Though they do not know one another at the outset, it turns out that both Conleth Doyle and Actaeon O'Neill are traveling to the same place: a tidal river town on the Slaney. Neither has seen this town in decades.

This work comprises six scenes and two voices: Conleth Doyle's and Actaeon's O'Neill's. In addition, as the reader will note, Conleth Doyle, and Actaeon O'Neill to a lesser extent, also serve as "omniscient" narrators. Their purpose is to provide background information on New Dawn Patriotism and the Great Removal that followed its rise—all following the collapse of the economic system and civil society in Ireland.

As they move forward from their seats toward the front of the bus, Actaeon O'Neill, who seems most fearful, links arms with Conleth Doyle. Conleth Doyle is the first to speak.

SCENE ONE

CONLETH DOYLE. First snowflakes, then freezing rain,
Finally layers of wheezing fog gather
To greet us on disembarkation at the
Riverside. Long ships and flat cots
Await us, and bearded sailors gathering
Sacks of grain. A line of lanterns leads
To a gangplank, shawled women rush
Panicked along the quayside to doors
Of jumping taverns, all white-hot havens
Of sedition. A dog barks on an old ship's
Prow. On the hills and roofs of my old
Hometown, I see matted grey snow

And on all trees menacing irons of ice.
Now, we must descend to bedlam from
This ordered stage. The bus pulls away
From Bus Line Shop as if to say, old men,
Your fates are here determined. I am
Conleth Doyle, driven many decades
From the fragrant avenues of this town.
Fearful, I am jostled by thin bodies blown
Toward me by waves of hate when I
Descend to quayside. Each face I greet
Is settled to a scowl, great power residing
In numbers after all. A runted child spits
Forward though the doorway of a dark-
Ened hall. I lived here once. My home
Looked across Hill Road to a little park
Where children liked to push friends
To greater heights on creaking swings.
Each morning we walked a narrow path
Between grey houses to primary school.

ACTAEON O'NEILL. I am Actaeon O'Neill, another native
Of this town and valley, from Br. Harris'
Tables, songs, canes, his compositions
Too but a single decade removed from
You. Here, we were many generations
A family of honest tailors who climbed
Hills each Sabbath to hear among our
Brethren the good news, who drove on
Summer days with mild dispatch to
Seaside dunes. I mark you now for a
Cousin of red-haired Billy Dunne: he
And I were seated side-by-side at school.
But I was never there: surely I imagined
It all. What transpired that fateful day
In the Miller's Field's can be counted
But a horrid, fitful, dark, and most awful
Waking dream. I will confront it now.

My brother, Conleth Doyle, if you will
Hear me out, I can be freed of this night-
Mare. Fearful and alone, I have returned
From our nation's capital this day. I am
Thankful for your company and calm.
Brother, hear my tale. I ask no more.

CONLETH DOYLE. Take a moment, my new companion,
To catch your breath before embarking
On this tale as, warily, we walk forward.
For safety and for traction too, we should
Link arms to climb the many steep hills
That lead to St. Ronan's Cathedral. At
Each step, we will feel our years. Indeed
It is a struggle to ascend: we are two old
Men returned to walk the streets of our
Hometown, taking advantage of the recent
Amnesty our government declared. Go on.

ACTAEON O'NEILL: From a copse's heart in the Miller's Field,
Close by the railway line, I thought
I heard running water and sweet tones
Of chanting girls. I can recall that it was
A humid day and cows were gathered
At a scratching post as I approached
The orchid, ash and hazel fronting that
Clump of trees. Beyond the copse's
Perimeter, many other layers of briar
And skeagh awaited me. But I persisted
Recalling all we had learned at school
From men as various as Br. Keegan
And Chips McGee. A tragic sequence
Of events was about to unfold: soon, I
Would be banished from town and family
By a pack of hounds. Then, the great
Catastrophe would befall our nation:
Civil society all broken down, banks

83

Boarded-up, laws enacted to hinder
My return. Until this hour, my story
Has not been told. Let us now link closer,
Conleth Doyle, I fear these agitators
Who roam as dogs through our old
Hometown. Of thugs we must be wary.

CONLETH DOYLE. Let's stop our walk to view the ruin of
Old Town Square. Look! Broken statuary
Many visitors had at one time strained
To view litters wide pedestals and white
Surrounding ground: here, a once-loved
Patriot lies pulverized while over there
I observe the sharpened edges of a busted
Holy man and scribe. A corps of sweepers
Weaves shards and dust about the Square
In widening gyres as I survey such
Cobbled spaces where, as a boy, I
Had often hid and played. From behind
The courthouse, acrid smoke ascends
To the wintry sky. I note two patrolmen
With louche address fiddling brown
Belts outside of Police HQ, as I cast
A furtive gaze about for one warm face
That I might recognize, walking onward,
Upward, and most wholly terrified.
Sensing my discomfort at this awful
Scene, my new companion, Actaeon
O'Neill, holds more tightly to my arm.

ACTAEON O'NEILL. At last, dear companion Conleth, the final
Bush and thorn yielded to my harsh
Address, revealing Diana naked: she spun
Slowly counter-clockwise on an ornate
Chandelier, attended to by nymph-like
Acolytes, the works that turned her pushed
By youths dressed-up in old militia gear.

Water cascaded down the chamber's walls,
Steam ascended fog-like toward the blazing
Lights atop the roof of that unusual place.
I stood transfixed at the curve of her
Behind, the firmness of her breasts,
The fierce darkness of her hair. Excited,
Wracked, tormented and aflame, I could
Make no effort to avert my gaze. Though,
I might say, for all of Diana's beauty,
There was something cheap and tacky
About the scene: it rang of some great
Falsehood I was quite unable to define.
I sensed, then, a redness glowing on my
Cheeks, my khakis bursting at their seams.
Diana! Do you not recall that wild and
Savage text from our secondary school?

CONLETH DOYLE. Be assured, I reply, I know it very well.
A terror that is with me still. End of Lower
Hall, Mr. Rigoberto Kelly's class, the day
He beat me black and blue: Nephele, Hyale,
Phiale, Psecas, and Rhanis with water filled
Great earthen jars before pouring evenly
Over Diana. Misspelling the penultimate
Acolyte's name, old Kelly struck me many
Times across my calves with an implement
He had dubbed his "Board of Education."
Upward then, his timber reached all ready
To address my waiting hands. I did not cry.
A slaughterhouse many called our school:
The Classics spread across our native land.
What odd times when myth assumes reality.

SCENE TWO

CONLETH DOYLE. I am Conleth Doyle, these four decades
Removed from this town, and four hard
Decades full of yearning for this return.
Actaeon O'Neill, we can rest easy now.
So long decrepit and gone so gray, notice
There is no one here who can recall
Our names. To think we are remembered
Would be an affectation. We have been
Erased from the oral history of the town.
Shameful how we had to leave, more
Shameful still how none can register
Today our belonging to these ancient
Streets that like blood flow through
Our veins. For days after the banks'
Collapse, decades ago, we went about
Our familiar routines. Can you recall
That early May's unseasonable heat?
Then, suddenly, mobs marauded daily.
Shops were emptied, schools closed,
With my colleagues I was dragged
From my Post Office counter and flung
Into a holding pen in Thomas Davis
Sq. With many hundreds, I was held
Under armed guard, the mob now
Officially formed into a high militia.
At night, we heard gunfire, screams,
Jeeps racing through the streets, while
On the air drifted news of burning
Timbers and the finest register of
Frenzied flesh, dark legends drifting
Nightly through the town. Late one
Evening, we were loaded into cattle
Cars, then transported to the capital
By train, the soft country air giving
Way to the city's harsher glare. Left

With little room to move, when one
Man asked of the toilet's exact location
He was beaten about his legs by roughs
Got up in uniform. On arrival, we
Were set to work with heavy freight
Near Lansley Bay. Among many
Thousand men, I slept in an iron cot
Inside a cold warehouse, eating grub
From rusty biscuit tins. We played
Cards at night while Davy Lynch
Strummed tunes on his banjo. We lived
Through the long nightmare of New
Dawn Patriotism, that grand title our
New outfit of governance, in all
Importance to be sure, claimed as its
Inheritance, handed down from dead
Generations, long buried in our ancient
Soil. Many faceless men emerged
From nighttime shadows: they were
Fully armed and dangerous, our newest
Band of patriots taking up the cudgel
When our modern banks had failed.
Each night at the capital work camp
Was counted as a blank text I would
Not read. The country's population
Had been spread about by edict, we
Soon learned, so none could live
Among folk he or she might call his/
Her own. All were classed as
Strangers everywhere in this our old
Homeland, forced outward, sent away.
Now, the iron grip has loosened some:
New Dawn Patriotism, like much that
Rose before, has lost its thrust. A sort
Of glasnost has emerged that will allow
Us to regain some dinnseanchas briefly
Of families long lost and all dispersed.

Actaeon, Companion, we have ventured
To our old hometown: we are careful,
Vigilant, foolish, wholly heartbroken.

ACTAEON O'NEILL. For my part, I should remind you now,
Those events that hastened my departure
Occurred at a time some months previous
To your own though I, like many, noted
Winds of change in citizens' faces, heard
From mouths the foulest words, glimpsed
Often though private windows shadows
Of arms raised to strike elderly and child
Alike. Our citizens had heaped porcelain
And merchandise throughout their homes
So that it grew impossible to walk from
Room to room in each and every house
That formed the town. Constantly, we
Observed the rush to National Airport
Where thousands boarded jets to seek
Even shinier objects overseas. We knew
A crunch must come and soon it did
Occur. Banks failing, salaries unpaid,
Little of public funds were spread around
To ease the pain. As soon as foodstuffs
Appeared at Tesco, crowds descended
From the hills to loot the shelves for
Many had grown desperate, and with
Fierce hungers raged. Parents who seek
To feed their young should not be held
To negative account. To America they
Had fled, our government of rogues,
To kick heels in Miami's beach-side
Bars among dictators and sundry king-
Pins of illegal trades. As you said,
A new militia emerged to restore order
In the months after I had gone. Raised
With few of our minority faith, we

Have been trained to listen for what-
Ever of dissonance is carried forward
On the wind. Eyes open all the time.

CONLETH DOYLE. Yes, Actaeon, I remember now. Your
Heritage is mixed. With your brothers
You attended the Christian Brothers
School while worshipping Sundays
Among the Protestants at St. John's.

ACTAEON O'NEILL. Correct. In my youth, I gathered from
Two faiths all that was best: in this town
That was to me a sacred space. Until
A dramatic and most personal event
Forced me out. I found my way
To the capital where I hid and worked
Anonymously among relatives. I am
Fully rested. Let's go onward now,
My friend. This brief, cold, winter's day.

SCENE THREE

CONLETH DOYLE. Eerie to observe the quiet of the town,
How little of traffic passes, how hard
A familiar street will resound bereft
Of children's play. Women slink in
And out of shops, each huddled to near
Invisibility by tight-wound scarves
And gray overcoats. Like serpents, rolls
Of fog thickly curl around them. Men
Are nowhere to be seen, shelves seem
Nearly empty save for some canned
Goods, many businesses have been
Boarded-up. Winds gust up and down
Main St., the fog itself appears as if it is
About to shake. Blocks of ice crash
Earthward to the footpaths, big chunks
Of ice are gathered at the shores. In the
Cathedral garden, we notice on our
Approach, between curbside and
The grand entry to St. Ronan's, how
A burned-out BMW rests on top of
Bishop Dolan's tomb. We enter
The cathedral. I was baptized here,
I say to my companion. All belonging
To me have worshipped here. As if
Some awful Cromwellian return had
Taken place, we face a sacred site
Devoid of icon, symbol, or even stick
Of furniture. In the centre of a nave,
Two rusted cement lorries idle, their
Drivers feasting on huge mounds of
Sandwiches. Litter is strewn about
While the fine stained glass windows,
The work of Evie Hone, have been
Removed, or smashed, so that a fierce
Gale races through. Great icicles drop

Downward through the shades, the roof
Fully open to the skies. From the cracked
Marble baptismal font, emerges stench
Of piss and putrid fecal shite. I flee
Enraged by such an awful sight and tell
My companion I do not wish to linger
A moment longer in our hellish town.

ACTAEON O'NEILL. Wait! Let us walk a little farther before
Departing. I have brought a modest
Picnic. Please share my food with me?

CONLETH DOYLE. Actaeon, reaching into the deep pockets
Of his coat, brings out ham sandwiches
And a bag of fruit. Disarmed, I walk
Across the street to take away two cups
Of tea from Giovanni's, the red chipper
Of pitched battles after the discos of my
Youth, and bring them to the Fair Green
Where Actaeon has found some decent
Shelter hard by the ruin of a bungalow.
From Nolan's Tavern, raucous voices
Are carried on the wind. Though we
Would enjoy beer in the warm indoors,
We are fearful of who might know us
Were we to cross to there from the out-
Of-doors. The sad decades has left us
Shaken: clearly, none cares a holy hoot
To remember us. Quickly, we finish off
Our lunch and invent a plan to walk
The perimeter of the town that will allow,
Where streets converge, a wider view
Of the dim activity taking place this day.
As we take off, a corps of schoolboys
Overtakes us as they grimly parade
To the pebble-dashed walls of the CBS,
All expecting further beatings to endure,

The corporal punishment ban being long
Repealed. Soon, revived by walking, I ask
Actaeon to deliver a sharp conclusion
To his tale. I am anxious to know how
It came to end. Slowing pace, he resumes.

ACTAEON O'NEILL. Great roars erupted when the acolytes
Discovered me. The women rushed
To shield Diana's nakedness while
Boys in uniform called out, "The Dogs,
The Dogs." Then, a deep silence fell
That made me conscious of many angry
Eyes leering to where I crouched.
I heard water trickle down the interior
Walls of this most private space which
In error, to my great regret, I had, in folly,
Violated. Held captive by that gaze,
I felt a throbbing metamorphosis to my
Self. I had now begun to assume another
Shape: I shrank toward the ground, legs
And arms contracting, my ears growing
Outward. Hair began to sprout where
None had grown before. My heartbeat
Quickened and, though too terrified
To examine in great detail, I could sense
Myself transformed into a hare. Then,
I heard the pack's roar. Looking across
At them when they had been called
To heel, I recognized many dogs I had
Befriended at the County Greyhound
Track when I had lingered there along-
Side Gerard Kelly as he took a final
Look before wagering a bet. Instinctively,
As if I were possessed of ancient power,
The dogs would look my way as they
Were paraded, and seek to inhale
Odors attached to my flesh and clothes.

Wherever I stood, they would one
Moment pause, then allow themselves
Be walked round the ring another time.
It was clear that these greyhounds
Disliked to race and liked the violence
Of coursing even less: they conveyed
As much to me. Among the regulars
Of punters at the track, this play between
The hounds and I had grown into stuff
Of legend. I was often pointed out,
The young pulling parents to my side.
Once, Jem Kyle with pen and paper
Appeared at my front door to write my
Story up for the *Weekly News*. Many
Of these hounds that faced me in Diana's
Secret place I knew by name: Garden
Mews, Colonial Boy, Carrigeen Head,
Meadow Pipit, Shadow Song, twice
Winner of the Grand Prize, Whispering
Wind, and Campile Rocket were among
Those hounds I found time to recognize.
But it was a sad, irregular and most
Confusing scene, for fifty dogs or more
Were wildly tethered to the voice of man.
Dogs I had known as friends, now all
Meant harm to me. Then, a single voice
Released the hounds. Armed with the old
Instinct of the hare, in terror I took off.
Bolting toward the entryway of Diana's
Bathing pool, I crashed headlong into
A pile of sticks that caused a great
Collapse of logs and earth, the knock-on
Effect of this disorder slowing the pack
Of greyhounds down, handlers having to
Push through gaps for them to resume
The chase. I tore across the Miller's Field,
Headed for the river, at my back the barks

Of dogs, the roars of men. Though a hare,
Fast to run, it was struggle to adjust my
Brain to this new gait. The hounds caught
Me where the Bann and Slaney meet:
Under the shadow, cold and dreary,
Of the iron railway bridge. Immediately,
I felt the sharpened canine teeth dig
Into skin, cartilage and bone, saw hare's
Blood spurt to grass, and felt throughout
My body the most excruciating pain
Shuttle everywhere. As their teeth were
About to fasten about my throat, I called
Out to them: I am Actaeon O'Neill—
Remember me, your old companion from
The County Greyhound Track. Often,
You said to me as you were sent out
On parade before a race that no ill-will
Did you bear onto the hare. You told
Me that you had been trained to violence
By men. Now, you have been pressed
Into a killing pack, called to murder one
You had called your friend. Old Shadow
Song and your companions, please show
Some touch of mercy onto me. Suddenly,
The barking ceased, teeth released their
Savage grips. For a moment, hesitating,
I froze. Then hearing the hunters' voices—
The men's and not the dogs'—I raced
Headlong into the Bann, floating quickly
To the Slaney, then, on the current and
Ebbing tide, downward toward the sea.
Shadow Song's final words remain with
Me. We are driven to madness by the age.
Friend, please forgive for our awful rage.

SCENE FOUR

CONLETH DOYLE. Walking the parched perimeter of the town,
We note the famed museum is now a ruin
And public buildings everywhere show
Evidence of arson. Hearing a loud roar on
Oldcastle Road, we hide behind a brown
Container and from our place of concealment
Observe what we most fear—hunters
Bearing cudgels who roam the town as gangs.
Though the revolution's bubble has burst
And a peace had been agreed, rogue elements
Have power and passion still to terrorize.
From all classes and professions, these thugs
Are drawn, their poison attracts the young
And old alike. I light a cigarette and ponder
Actaeon's revelations. Though hard to credit,
His story has the ring of credibility for all
Its variance from the facts they pummeled
Into us at national school. Feeling safe again,
We walk downhill to view again the river
That defines the town as we wind our way
Toward the quay where in an hour it will
Be time to depart by bus. Unsettled by
Wind and gaining tide, waters snap angrily
At air while a weak light fights to hold
A foothold near the reeds. A lone blue
Heron adds definition to the scene. Southward,
I note that the great oaks of Cullen's Wood
Have been felled. And looking north, it is
Clear that the limestone overlook has been
Blasted into sand. I think of sun and moon,
A once connected world, of all my family
Who have lived and died and loved this river,
And whose last rites I was, by state prevention,

Unable to attend. I curse our government
And state. Actaeon, my friend, the harshest
Punishment is to be sent abroad from your
Own place. We are but dead men here.
Let's move on. Heeding me, Actaeon,
Clears his throat, then resumes his tale.

ACTAEON O'NEILL. Sinking downward, I grew certain that
I would die by drowning. I was in pain
And shock and knew that I was bleeding
Everywhere. Darkness of great depth
Descended down as sunlight lost for me
Its stable register in the sky. Then, pike
Allowed me to break my fall: underwater,
Like a line of sleepers holding-up one
Steel rail, I was propped in place then
Stabilized. With most smooth alignment,
The pike turned clockwise as a team:
Thereby suspending me firmly in place.
Again, I could see above the river's
Surface a bright sun, and learned while
Lying flat that I had been given ability
To breathe in water. Next, as if I had
Been placed on one of those most ancient
Wracks on which our ancestors were
By Saxons stretched, I felt my body
Being pulled into its former shape,
The greater length and bulk—conversion
From hare to human being—calling forth
Taut pike in even greater numbers. From
Every place beneath the Slaney's surface
Trout and salmon arrived to mark approval
Of the unfolding scene. About my arms
And legs I felt dabs' caresses and then,
To my delight, many eels addressed my
Wounds, which, once I had been restored
To my former shape, had erupted into pain

Of fierce intensity. Gently, they sucked
Poison from my sores before gliding away.
Soon, many shellfish, crabs and crayfish
As I suspect, emerged to stitch the open
Wounds the eels had cleansed. Finally,
An otter appeared to supervise the scene
And in short order did declaim me healed.

CONLETH DOYLE. St. Catherine of Siena performed miracles.
We learned of her deeds while on retreat,
How she cured the sick by sucking poisons
From their sores and battle wounds. Your
Story brings me back to childhood days.
I doubt not the veracity of your narrative.

ACTAEON O'NEILL. So, Conleth, I floated downriver toward
Wexford on the tide. I clung to a tree limb,
Avoiding snags as they appeared, racing
Smoothly through an isolated whirlpool
Or two as I flew, quicker than you would
Imagine, between our home place and the
County town we have long-held in low
Regard. A flock of guillemots guided me
Through the harbor to a fishing boat: I
Climbed stealthily on board and among
A cluster of lobster pots concealed myself.
Past midnight, the vessel headed outbound
For Howth where I disembarked and made
My way by DART to live these lost decades
Among relatives, near the old infirmary.

SCENE FIVE

CONLETH DOYLE. These strange and troubled times have
Handed down an opulence of stories,
Yours hardly the strangest I have heard
Related. Eerie how myth and history can
Be repeated and wildly interchanged, your
Life becomes a story taught violently at
School. The capital we did not approve
Of—we are honest countrymen after all—
Concealed us. We could hide. We might
Mingle among crowds, identities concealed.
Not too hard we soon learned: our leaders
Did not bother often with the nuts and bolts
Of government: little account was made of
Who went where and when, and names
In prison camps were seldom written down.
Leaders and minions liked instead to amass
Great piles of junk in their living rooms
And yards. Their most idle hours were spent
At confiscations and inventories of stolen
Goods. Like air released from a balloon,
However, the ages of avarice, greed and
Gross stupidity did subside. Foreign agencies
Stepped inside our territory and eased all
Bloated rebels aside, so we now await
The return of our exiled government
From Florida, that shower of jumped-up
Johnnies tanned and fat from feasting
Daily on the flesh of grouper and juices
Of mimosas. I hear the old leader has
Found true love in the arms of an aged
Movie star, that he longs to kiss our holy
Ground on his return. Though, as we
Have seen today, gangs linger. We are
Free again, if only to note what is lost.

ACTAEON O'NEILL. Great debts I owe to pike, salmon, trout,
Eels, and all fine creatures of the river,
And fair birds and fowl that served
To guide me safely on. But, we should
Walk onward to the quay. Our time in
Town grows short, our bus will depart
For Dublin in another hour or so. Let's go.

SCENE SIX

CONLETH DOYLE. Linking arms as we walk on, we find
No further impulse to confess. Then,
Turning left, we meet the promenade
Where the path cuts between the razed
Hotel and litter-strewn Pearse playground.
Each bench we pass is empty of old men:
A gnarled line of youths has gathered
Underneath an evergreen. Crossing
Furlong Bridge to Bus Line Shop,
Dodging angry crowds, including ranks
Of emaciated girls and boys, we notice
Danny Jones, long-time mayor of our old
Hometown, pissing fully toward a golden
Watering can. The chef's hat he wears
Gives his post away: MAYOR blazoned
In boldest colours to his crown. Outside
A drapery and pizza shop combined, we
Observe a group of men pile clothes
On top of battered library books into
A burning skip. Girls fling bottles river-
Ward at a wounded cygnet separated
From its herd. Two shawled women just
Evicted from a bar are going at it
Tooth and nail, a large crowd gathering
To encourage the brutal scene. On a
Bench, a meitheal of men and boys pass
Cans of cider and medications back and
Forth, hand to hand, as sullen dockers
Unload cargo from wooden cots. We,
Two old men, worn-out, exiled four
Decades from the town, await the arrival
Of our bus; all the while, Actaeon is
Staring at his feet. From the shop,
Against the rigours of the road, I have
Bought bags of Taytos and bottles of

Good Lucozade. We climb to the safety
Of the bus. Once seated, Actaeon closes
His eyes. I watch the waters' headlong
Surge under bridges, their need to leave
As urgent as my own, and I notice too,
On a river island, ponies gathered near
The gable of a ruined shed sheltering from
A sharp freezing rain that has begun to fall.
We are headed northward toward our
Capital. Actaeon O' Neill is fast asleep.

NOTES

"The Found World" was inspired by Robin Robertson's "The Wood of Lost Things" from *The Wrecking Light*, Picador Poetry, 2010. To indicate how one poem took flight from another, a few phrases at the beginning of "The Found World" have been borrowed from Robertson's poem. Seabhac mara (sea-hawk). Fuiseóg (skylark). Préachán dubh (rook). Géis (swan). Gabhlán gaoithe (swift). Caislín dearg (stonechat).

"A Life of Pat the Scruff, Chapter 12." John Ashcroft was Governor of Missouri from 1985-1993 and US Attorney General from 2001-2005. He is also a noted composer and singer of religious songs. Stephen Stills, "Love the One You're With." *Stephen Stills.* Atlantic, 1970.

"The Pilgrims Emerge from the Forest." St. Senan (c. 488-544) founded Enniscorthy, Co. Wexford, in 510.

"Aubade Cracked Along the Edges of Iowa." *Oku-no-hosomichi* is *Narrow Road to the Interior.* "The images themselves, true to Chinese literary Zen pedagogy, arise naturally out of the *hsin* (Japanese: *kokoro*), the heart-soul-mind of the poet". Sam Hamill trans. *Narrow Road to the Interior.* Boston & London: Shambala Publications, 1991.

"A Sort of Crusade". Raymond Burke served as Catholic Archbishop of St. Louis from 2003-2008. A controversial figure, he preached during the 2004 presidential election (John Kerry v George W. Bush) that Catholics such as Kerry who supported legalized abortion should not be allowed to receive communion—a not-so-subtle hint that Catholics should vote Republican.

"Snow Falling on Opening Day." Albert Pujols and Adam Wainwright play for the St. Louis Cardinals baseball team.

"Sailing Lake Mareotis." Books referred to include William Least-Heat Moon. *PrairyErth.* Boston: Houghton-Mifflin, 1991. Michael Haag. *Alexandria: City of Memory.* New Haven: Yale UP, 2004. El Clásico is the title given to soccer matches between Real Madrid and Barcelona. Javier Mascherano (Argentina) plays for Barcelona.

"Actaeon's Return." For further information on this turbulent period in Irish history, readers should consult the many books that *B. F. Wacker* has written on the subject. Her next volume, *Thugocracy: The Rise and Fall of New Dawn Patriotism in Ireland*, will be published next year by Gargoyle University Press. Further information on Actaeon can be found in Ted Hughes. *Tales from Ovid.* London: Faber and Faber, 1997.

A native of Enniscorthy, Co. Wexford, EAMONN WALL was educated at University College Dublin, the University of Wisconsin-Milwaukee, and the City University of New York, where he received a Ph.D. in English.

Eamonn Wall's poetry and prose have been included in anthologies in Ireland and the United States including *The Book of Irish-American Poetry from the 18th Century to the Present*; *Irish Writing in the Twentieth Century: a Reader*; *Wexford Through its Writers*; *Flood Stage: An Anthology of St. Louis Poets*; and *The Big Empty: Contemporary Nebraska Nonfiction Writers*.

Essays, articles, and reviews of Irish, Irish American, and American writers have appeared in *The Irish Times, New Hibernia Review, Irish Literary Supplement, The Washington Post, Chicago Tribune, South Carolina Review*, and other journals.

Through his involvement in the Launchpad and Scallta Media initiatives, which he helped set up to encourage the development of young writers and artists in Co. Wexford, he has continued to play a role in the artistic life of Co. Wexford. Eamonn Wall lives in Missouri, where he teaches at the University of Missouri-St. Louis.

Eamonn Wall's website is www.eamonnwall.net.